# Count Your Way through
# Afghanistan

by **Jim Haskins** and **Kathleen Benson**

illustrations by **Megan Moore**

**M** Millbrook Press / Minneapolis

To Josh and Jem Dyson  –K. B.

To my parents, Ron and Barbara.
Thank you for all your support.  –M. M.

Text copyright © 2007 by Jim Haskins and Kathleen Benson
Illustrations copyright © 2007 by Millbrook Press, Inc.

Millbrook Press, Inc.
A division of Lerner Publishing Group
241 First Avenue North
Minneapolis, Minnesota 55401 U.S.A.

Website address: www.lernerbooks.com

Library of Congress Cataloging-in-Publication Data

Haskins, James, 1941–
    Count your way through Afghanistan / by Jim Haskins and
Kathleen Benson ; illustrations by Megan Moore.
        p.   cm. — (Count your way)
    ISBN-13: 978–1–57505–880–1 (lib. bdg. : alk. paper)
    ISBN-10: 1–57505–880–4 (lib. bdg. : alk. paper)
    1. Afghanistan—Civilization—Juvenile literature.  2. Pushto
language—Numerals—Juvenile    literature.  3.  Counting—
Juvenile literature.  I. Benson, Kathleen. II. Moore, Megan, ill.
III. Title.
DS354.H37 2007
958.1—dc22                                          2005033173

Manufactured in the United States of America
1  2  3  4  5  6  –  DP  –  12  11  10  09  08  07

# Introduction

The country of Afghanistan is located in central Asia. It has an area of 251,773 square miles. It is slightly smaller than Texas. More than 28 million people live in Afghanistan. Afghanistan has two official languages: Dari and Pashto. Dari is similar to Farsi, which is spoken in Iran. Many Afghans speak Dari and Pashto. Both languages use the Arabic alphabet. This alphabet is read from right to left. We will count through Afghanistan in Pashto.

**1** ) (yao)

Afghanistan has **one** Blue Mosque. It is covered with many tiny blue and white tiles. The Blue Mosque is one of the most famous mosques in the country. A mosque is an Islamic place of worship. Nearly all Afghans follow the religion of Islam. Religion is a very important part of Afghan life.

# 2 ٢ (dwa)

**Two** paddles toss wheat into the air. This process is called winnowing. Winnowing separates the wheat from the chaff. Chaff covers the wheat while it is on the plant. People do not eat the chaff. The wheat can be made into flour after it is separated from the chaff. Wheat is a key crop in Afghanistan.

# 3 ٣ (dray)

Afghanistan's flag has **three** stripes.
At the center is a white coat of arms.
It shows a wreath of wheat surrounding
a mosque. Above the mosque are the
words, "There is no God but Allah and
Muhammad is the Prophet of Allah" and
"God is Almighty." Muhammad was the
founder of Islam. This has been the
official flag of Afghanistan since 2004.

# 4 ٤ (tsa-lore)

**Four** women wear *burkas* (ber-KUHZ).
Many Afghan women wear this large
piece of clothing.  Men and women in
Afghanistan believe that everyone
should cover themselves and dress
modestly.  Some women wear a scarf on
their head instead of a burka.  Men
often wrap long pieces of cloth around
their heads.  These are called turbans.

# 5 0 (pin-ZAY)

A trader leads **five** camels through the Khyber Pass. This very old road connects Afghanistan and Pakistan. The Khyber Pass cuts through the Safed Koh mountain range. Armies, explorers, and traders have traveled this road for hundreds of years.

# 6 7 (shpag)

Afghanistan shares borders with **six** countries. They are China, Pakistan, Iran, Turkmenistan, Uzbekistan, and Tajikistan. Afghanistan is landlocked. That means it is surrounded by land on all sides.

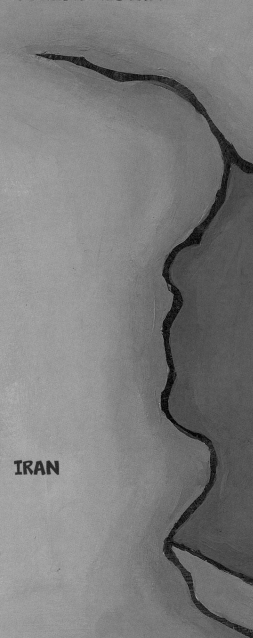

IRAN

# 7 ۷ (wuh)

**Seven** Afghans pass by the Darulaman Palace. An Afghan king built this palace. Afghanistan has had a lot of wars and fighting in the past 25 years. These battles almost destroyed the palace. But there is hope for the future. Afghanistan's new government plans to repair the building. It will become the home of the parliament. Members of the parliament are elected to make the country's laws.

# 8 人 (a-TAY)

A man displays **eight** rugs at an outdoor
market.  Afghans have practiced the art
of rug making for hundreds of years.
They use wool to weave the rugs.
Sometimes they also use goat hair or
camel hair.  Plants and insects are
used to create some of the dyes
for the colorful rugs.

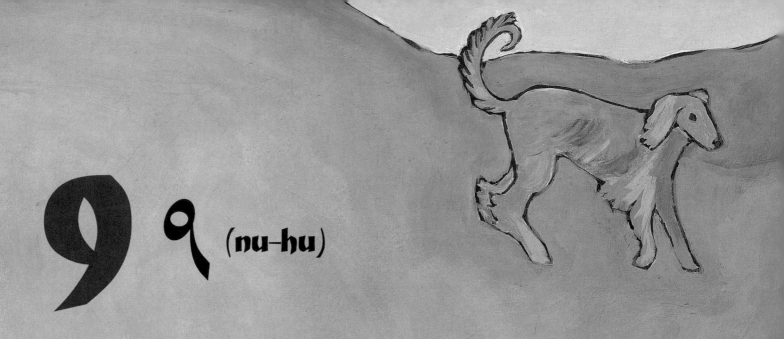

**9** ٩ **(nu–hu)**

An Afghan hound guards **nine** sheep.
Afghan hounds can run, leap, and turn on
hilly land.  Afghan shepherds use these
dogs to protect their sheep from wolves.

Afghanistan is especially known for its
karakul sheep.  These animals have long,
silky fleece.  The skins of lambs are
sometimes made into hats and coats.

# 10 ١٠ (lahs)

**Ten** kites fly in the sky. In Afghanistan, kites are used for the sport of kite fighting. Kids and adults glue crushed glass to their kite strings. Then they try to cut the strings of other kites. Kite flyers must wear gloves to protect their hands. If they lose a fight, they may lose their kite forever.

# Pronunciation Guide

1 / ١ / yao

2 / ٢ / dwa

3 / ٣ / dray

4 / ٤ / tsa-lore

5 / ٥ / pin-ZAY

6 / ٦ / shpag

7 / ٧ / wuh

8 / ٨ / a-TAY

9 / ٩ / nu-hu

10 / ١٠ / lahs